RANJOT SINGH CHAHAL

English Punctuation Made Easy

A Step-by-Step Guide to Mastering English Punctuation

Rana Books

Contents

Introduction

Punctuation is the system of symbols and marks used in writing to clarify meaning indicate pauses and help structure sentences and paragraphs. It plays a crucial role in conveying the intended tone rhythm and emphasis of written language. Without punctuation written texts may become confusing or difficult to understand. It helps to differentiate between different types of sentences such as questions exclamations or statements and guides readers on how to interpret and read them. Punctuation marks include various symbols like commas periods question marks exclamation points colons semicolons quotation marks and parentheses among others. By using punctuation effectively writers can enhance clarity coherence and overall impact in their writing.

1.1 Understanding the Role of Punctuation

Punctuation plays a crucial role in writing as it helps to structure sentences and convey meaning effectively. It acts as a guide for readers indicating where to pause emphasize certain words or phrases and understand the relationships between different parts of a sentence.

One of the primary functions of punctuation is to provide clarity by marking the boundaries of different elements in a sentence. For example commas are used to separate items in a list clauses in a sentence or to set off non-essential information. Without the appropriate use of commas the meaning of a sentence can be altered or misunderstood.

Punctuation marks like periods question marks and exclamation marks are used at the end of sentences to indicate the intended tone or purpose of a statement. Periods signify a definitive end while question marks indicate a question being asked and exclamation marks convey excitement or strong emotions.

Other important punctuation marks include colons semicolons and hyphens. Colons are used to introduce a list or provide further explanation while semicolons help to connect related but separate ideas. Hyphens are used to join words together or to indicate the division of a word at the end of a line.

Understanding the appropriate use of punctuation is crucial for effective communication in writing. It ensures that the intended meaning is conveyed accurately and helps to enhance the overall readability and coherence of a piece of writing. Therefore mastering the rules of punctuation is essential for any writer who seeks to communicate clearly.

1.2 Enhancing Clarity and Meaning in Writing

Enhancing clarity and meaning in writing is essential for effectively conveying ideas and engaging readers. Strong writing skills not only rely on sound grammar and vocabulary but also on the ability to communicate ideas in a clear concise and coherent manner.

One way to enhance clarity in writing is to use precise and specific language. Instead of using vague or general terms opting for precise words can provide a better understanding of the intended message. Additionally eliminating unnecessary words or phrases can help streamline the writing and make it more concise.

Another technique that can enhance clarity is organizing ideas in a logical structure. Writers can use paragraphs and headings to break down information and provide a clear flow of ideas. This helps readers to follow the argument or narrative easily and understand the connections between different points.

Furthermore using transitional words and phrases can improve the coherence of a piece of writing. These words and phrases help to establish relationships between different sentences and paragraphs making the writing more cohesive and ensuring a smooth transition from one idea to the next.

Proofreading and editing are crucial steps in enhancing clarity and meaning in writing. Reviewing the text for grammatical errors ambiguous phrasing or awkward sentence structures can greatly improve the overall quality of the writing. It allows writers to identify areas for improvement and make necessary revisions to ensure the message is communicated effectively.

In summary enhancing clarity and meaning in writing involves understanding and utilizing proper punctuation using precise and specific language organizing ideas logically incorporating transitional words and proofreading and editing the text. By implementing these strategies writers can improve their communication skills and develop writing that is clear meaningful and engaging for readers.

1.3 Indicating Pauses and Rhythms

Punctuation plays a crucial role in indicating pauses and rhythms in writing. It helps the reader to navigate through the text smoothly and understand the intended meaning. For example consider the following sentence:

"Let's eat Grandma!"

Without punctuation the sentence can be interpreted as an urgent invitation to eat with Grandma. However when proper punctuation is used it becomes clear that it is a suggestion to Grandma saying "Let's eat" rather than "Let's eat Grandma!"

1.4 Conveying Emphasis and Tone

Punctuation also helps in conveying emphasis and tone in writing. By using punctuation marks such as exclamation points question marks and even ellipses writers can indicate excitement curiosity hesitation or other emotions. For example:

"What?! Are you serious?"

The use of an exclamation mark and a question mark conveys surprise and disbelief emphasizing the intensity of the speaker's reaction.

1.5 Differentiating Clauses and Sentence Structures

Punctuation is essential for differentiating clauses and sentence structures helping to clarify the relationship between ideas. For instance:

"I went to the store; then I met my friend."

By using a semicolon the writer clearly shows a connection between going to the store and meeting the friend indicating that both actions are related.

1.6 Creating Lists and Direct Speech

Punctuation is also used to create lists and mark direct speech in writing. For example:

"Please buy apples oranges and grapes."

The comma is used to separate each item in the list ensuring clarity and preventing confusion.

1.7 Avoiding Ambiguity and Misinterpretation

Punctuation helps prevent ambiguity and misinterpretation by clarifying the intended meaning of a sentence. Consider the following example:

"Let's eat kids!"

Without punctuation it could be misinterpreted as an invitation to eat the children. However with the proper use of a comma it becomes clear that the speaker is inviting the kids to eat.

1.8 Importance of Punctuation in Academic Writing

In academic writing punctuation is crucial as it contributes to the overall professionalism and clarity of the work. It helps the reader follow the logical flow of ideas and understand complex concepts. Academic writing follows specific punctuation rules including the appropriate use of commas colons semicolons and dashes.

For example consider the following sentence from an academic paper:

"The study aimed to explore the impact of social media on teenagers' mental health: specifically it investigated the relationship between excessive social media usage and symptoms of anxiety and depression."

The use of the colon and the semicolon in this sentence clearly indicates the purpose of the study and the specific focus of the investigation.

1.9 Importance of Punctuation in Creative Writing

In creative writing punctuation is essential for creating the desired effect and conveying the author's unique style and voice. Creative writers often make deliberate choices in their use of punctuation to create rhythm emphasis and mood. They may use ellipses to create pauses or suspense and dashes to indicate interruptions or abrupt changes.

For example consider the following sentence from a novel:

"She stood at the edge of the cliff hesitating—should she jump or turn back?"

The use of the dash in this sentence creates a moment of hesitation and suspense adding to the dramatic tension of the scene.

2. Enhancing Clarity and Meaning in Writing

2.1 Avoiding Run-on Sentences

Punctuation helps avoid run-on sentences which occur when two or more independent clauses are not properly separated. Run-on sentences can be confusing and make it difficult for the reader to understand the intended meaning. Correct punctuation eliminates ambiguity and helps the reader follow the flow of ideas.

For example consider the following run-on sentence:
   "I woke up early I had a big day ahead."
   By separating the two independent clauses with a period or using a coordinating conjunction and a comma the sentence becomes clearer:
   "I woke up early. I had a big day ahead."
   "I woke up early and I had a big day ahead."

2.2 Clarifying Sentence Structure
   Punctuation helps clarify sentence structure by indicating the relationships between different parts of a sentence. It helps the reader distinguish between main and subordinate clauses direct and indirect speech and various grammatical structures.

For example:
   "Although it was raining we decided to go for a walk."
   The use of a comma in this sentence clarifies that "Although it was raining" is an introductory clause introducing additional information about the weather condition.

2.3 Distinguishing Quotations and Dialogues
   Punctuation is crucial in distinguishing quotations and dialogues from the rest of the text. It helps indicate when someone is speaking or when a specific text is quoted. Quotation marks commas and other punctuation marks are used to enclose and separate dialogues and quotations.

For example:

John said "I'll be there at 6 pm."

The quotation marks and the comma clearly indicate that John is speaking and his statement overall effectiveness of written communication. Through its various roles punctuation enhances clarity indicates pauses and rhythms conveys emphasis and tone differentiates clauses and sentence structures creates lists and marks direct speech avoids ambiguity and misinterpretation and maintains consistency and coherence. Whether in academic writing or creative writing the proper use of punctuation is essential for effective communication and conveying the intended message.

Different Types of Punctuation Marks and Their Uses

2.1.1 Period (.)

The period is used to indicate the end of a sentence. For example: "I love to read books."

2.1.2 Question Mark (?)

The question mark is used to indicate a question. For example: "What time is it?"

2.1.3 Exclamation Mark (!)

The exclamation mark is used to indicate strong emotion or emphasis. For example: "I can't believe it!"

2.1.4 Comma (The comma is used to separate items in a list separate clauses in a sentence or indicate a pause. For example: "I need to buy apples bananas and oranges."

2.1.5 Colon (:)

The colon is used to introduce a list or to separate hours from minutes in time. For example: "My favorite fruits are: apples bananas and oranges."

2.1.6 Semicolon (;)

The semicolon is used to separate two independent clauses that are closely related. For example: "I love to read books; they take me to another world."

2.1.7 Dash (-)

The dash is used to indicate a sudden or dramatic change in thought or to introduce additional information. For example: "I bought some new shoes – they are so comfortable."

2.1.8 Quotation Marks (" ")

Quotation marks are used to indicate direct speech or to enclose titles of articles poems or chapters. For example: "He said 'I love you.'"

2.1.9 Parentheses ( )

Parentheses are used to provide additional information or to enclose an aside. For example: "The concert (which was amazing) lasted for three hours."

2.1.10 Apostrophe (')

The apostrophe is used to indicate possession contraction or to form plural possessive. For example: "Mary's car is red."

3. Enhancing Clarity and Meaning in Writing with Punctuation

Using punctuation correctly can greatly enhance the clarity and meaning of your writing. Let's consider some examples:

3.1 Ambiguity:
Without punctuation: "A woman without her man is nothing."
With punctuation: "A woman: without her man is nothing."
In the first example the absence of punctuation creates ambiguity suggesting that a woman is nothing without a man. However adding a colon and a comma in the second example clarifies that both woman and man are important.

3.2 Emphasis:
Without punctuation: "I can't believe he said that"
With punctuation: "I can't believe he said that!"
The addition of an exclamation mark emphasizes the speaker's shock or disbelief.

3.3 Different Meanings:
Without punctuation: "Let's eat Grandma!"
With punctuation: "Let's eat Grandma!"
Using a comma before "Grandma" indicates that the speaker is addressing Grandma inviting her to eat with them. However without a comma it suggests that the speaker is expressing their intent to eat Grandma.

In conclusion punctuation plays a vital role in English writing by clarifying meaning indicating pauses and emphasis and differentiating between different types of information. Understanding and using punctuation correctly can greatly enhance the effectiveness and clarity of your writing.

The Full Stop (Period)

2.1 Usage and Placement of Full Stops

The full stop also known as a period is one of the most common punctuation marks used in writing. Its primary function is to mark the end of a sentence. Understanding its usage and placement is crucial for clear and effective communication.

A full stop is used at the end of a declarative sentence which makes a statement or expresses a fact. For example:

- "I love to read."
    - "She has a beautiful voice."
    - "They live in New York."

Full stops are also used at the end of imperative sentences which give commands or make requests. For example:

- "Please close the door."
    - "Take a seat."
    - "Bring me a glass of water."

Additionally full stops are used at the end of sentences that are exclamatory expressing strong emotions or excitement. For example:

- "What a beautiful sunset!"
    - "I can't believe I won the lottery!"
    - "Congratulations on your promotion!"

2.2 Differentiating Between Abbreviations and Acronyms

Another important aspect of using full stops is differentiating between abbreviations and acronyms. Abbreviations are shortened versions of words or phrases usually formed by truncating letters. An abbreviation can be pronounced letter by letter or as a word. In British English it is common to use a full stop after each abbreviated word whereas in American English the full stop is typically omitted unless it is the last letter of the abbreviation. Here are a few examples:

- B.C. (British Columbia)
    - etc. (et cetera)
    - Mr. (Mister)
    - Dr. (Doctor)

On the other hand acronyms are formed by taking the initial letters of a series of words and pronouncing them as a word. Acronyms are not typically followed by a full stop unless it is used to avoid confusion or in a particular writing style. Here are examples of acronyms:

- NASA (National Aeronautics and Space Administration)

- FIFA (Fédération Internationale de Football Association)
- UNESCO (United Nations Educational Scientific and Cultural Organization)

It's important to note that different style guides and contexts may have specific rules regarding full stops with abbreviations and acronyms so it's always advisable to follow the appropriate guidelines.

Mastering the usage and placement of full stops is essential for clear and effective writing. It helps to separate ideas create coherence and ensure that readers can understand and interpret the intended message accurately.

The Comma

The comma is a versatile punctuation mark that is used to provide separation and pause in sentences. It serves several purposes in writing including indicating a pause for clarity separating items in a list introducing additional information and separating coordinate adjectives. However it is important to use commas correctly to avoid common errors.

3.1 Using Commas for Separation and Pause

One of the primary functions of the comma is to provide separation and pause in sentences. Commas are typically used to separate different elements within a sentence to enhance clarity and avoid confusion.

For example in the sentence "John went to the store and bought milk bread and eggs commas are used to separate the items in the list of groceries. Without the commas the sentence would be unclear and confusing.

Another common use of the comma for separation is when combining two independent clauses with a coordinating conjunction such as "and "but or "or." For instance "She went to the store and he stayed home." In this sentence the comma separates the two independent clauses providing a pause between them.

Additionally commas can be used to separate introductory phrases or clauses from the main clause. For example "After finishing his homework John went for a walk." The comma separates the introductory phrase "after finishing his homework" from the main clause "John went for a walk."

3.2 Avoiding Common Comma Errors

While commas are essential for clarity and proper sentence structure they can also cause confusion if used incorrectly. Here are some common comma errors to avoid:

1. Missing Comma with Coordinate Adjectives: When two or more adjectives modify the same noun a comma should be placed between them. For example "She had a long tiring day." Without the comma the sentence may imply that the day was both long and tiring.

2. Misplaced Comma with Restrictive and Non-Restrictive Clauses: A restrictive clause provides essential information about the noun it modifies and should not be separated by commas. On the other hand a non-restrictive clause provides additional non-essential information and should be separated by commas. For instance "The book that I borrowed from the library is overdue." Here the restrictive clause "that I borrowed from the library" is not separated by commas. In contrast in the sentence "My favorite book which I borrowed from the library

is overdue the non-restrictive clause "which I borrowed from the library" is set off by commas.

3. Comma Splice: A comma splice occurs when two independent clauses are connected by a comma without a coordinating conjunction. For example "I went to the store I bought some groceries." This error can be corrected by either adding a coordinating conjunction (e.g "I went to the store and I bought some groceries") or replacing the comma with a semicolon (e.g "I went to the store; I bought some groceries").

4. Comma After a Subordinating Conjunction: Subordinating conjunctions like "although "because and "while" introduce dependent clauses that cannot stand alone as complete sentences. Therefore a comma should not be placed after a subordinating conjunction. For example "Although it was raining we went for a walk." The comma after "Although" is incorrect and should be removed.

5. Overuse of Commas: Using too many commas can make a sentence sound choppy and confusing. It is important to only use commas where necessary for clarity and sentence structure. For instance "I went to the store and bought some milk bread and eggs on my way home from work." This sentence is overly punctuated and can be simplified to "I bought some milk bread and eggs on my way home from work."

In conclusion the comma is a versatile punctuation mark that provides separation and pause in sentences. It is essential to use commas correctly to enhance clarity and avoid common errors such as missing commas with coordinating adjectives misplaced commas with restrictive and non-restrictive clauses comma splices commas after subordinating conjunctions and the overuse of commas. By understanding the proper use of commas writers can effectively convey their thoughts and ideas while maintaining clear and concise sentences.

The Apostrophe

The apostrophe is a punctuation mark that serves multiple purposes in the English language. In this explanation we will focus on two main uses of the apostrophe: indicating possession and contraction/omission.

4.1 Indicating Possession:
   One of the primary uses of the apostrophe is to indicate possession. In this context the apostrophe is used to show that something belongs to someone or something else.

To indicate possession we generally add an apostrophe and the letter "s" ('s) to the noun that possesses another noun. However there are a few exceptions and variations to this rule.

Let's look at some examples to understand how the apostrophe is used to indicate possession:

1. Sarah's book
   - In this example the apostrophe is used to show that the book belongs to Sarah.

2. The dog's collar
  - Here the apostrophe indicates that the collar belongs to the dog.

3. My parents' house
  - In this case the apostrophe is placed after the "s" because the noun "parents" is already plural. The house belongs to both parents.

4. The students' notebooks
  - Similar to the previous example the apostrophe is placed after the "s" because the noun "students" is plural. The notebooks belong to multiple students.

5. The company's headquarters
  - Again the apostrophe is used to indicate that the headquarters belong to the company.

6. The child's toy
  - In this example the apostrophe indicates that the toy belongs to the child.

7. The doctor's appointment
  - Here the apostrophe shows that the appointment belongs to the doctor.

8. The country's flag
  - In this case the apostrophe indicates that the flag belongs to the country.

It's important to note that there are some special cases where the apostrophe is used differently when showing possession. For example:

- If the noun already ends in "s we add an apostrophe after the "s" without adding an extra "s."
   e.g James' car Jesus' teachings

- In the case of plural nouns that do not end in "s we add an apostrophe and "s" to indicate possession.
   e.g the women's bathroom the children's toys

4.2 Contraction and Omission:
   Another use of the apostrophe is to indicate contraction or omission in words and phrases. This involves combining two words and replacing the omitted letters with an apostrophe.

Contraction:
   In contractions the apostrophe is used to combine two words and indicate the omission of one or more letters. Here are some common examples:

1. I'm (I am)
   - The apostrophe replaces the "a" in "am." "I'm" is a contraction of "I am."

2. We'll (We will)
   - The apostrophe replaces the "wi" in "will." "We'll" is a contraction of "We will."

3. Don't (Do not)
   - The apostrophe replaces the "o" in "not." "Don't" is a

contraction of "Do not."

4. It's (It is)
   - The apostrophe replaces the "i" in "is." "It's" is a contraction of "It is."

Omission:
   In some cases the apostrophe is used to indicate the omission of letters without combining two words. Here are a few examples:

1. can't (cannot)
   - The apostrophe replaces the "no" in "cannot."

2. won't (will not)
   - The apostrophe replaces the "ill" in "will not."

3. I'd (I would)
   - The apostrophe replaces the "woul" in "would."

4. I've (I have)
   - The apostrophe replaces the "ha" in "have."

In addition to contractions and omissions the apostrophe is also used in certain abbreviations such as "can't" (short for "cannot") and "I've" (short for "I have").

It's important to use apostrophes correctly to avoid confusion and maintain proper grammar. Misusing or omitting apostrophes can change the meaning of a sentence or make it unclear.

In summary the apostrophe serves two main purposes: indicating possession and indicating contraction or omission. When used to indicate possession the apostrophe is placed before the "s" for singular nouns and after the "s" for plural nouns. In contractions and omissions the apostrophe is used to combine words or indicate the omission of letters. Proper use of apostrophes is important for conveying meaning accurately in written English.

The Question Mark and Exclamation Mark

5.1 Conveying Questions and Exclamations

The question mark and exclamation mark are punctuation marks that are used to convey questions and exclamations in written language. They help to add clarity and emphasis to the meaning of a sentence.

The question mark (?) is used at the end of a sentence to indicate that a question is being asked. It represents a rising intonation at the end of a sentence indicating that the sentence is meant to be understood as a question rather than a statement.

For example:
- "What is your name?"
- "Did you finish your homework?"
- "Where are you going?"

In these examples the question mark is used to indicate that the sentences are asking for information or seeking a response.

On the other hand the exclamation mark (!) is used at the end of a sentence to indicate strong emotion or a sense of excitement or surprise. It represents a sharp and sudden rise in intonation conveying an exclamatory tone.

For example:
 - "What a beautiful sunset!"
 - "I can't believe it!"
 - "Congratulations!"

In these examples the exclamation mark is used to emphasize the strong feelings or emotions being expressed in the sentences.

5.2 Proper Usage and Placement

While the question mark and exclamation mark are straightforward in their purpose it is important to use them correctly and place them appropriately in a sentence. Here are some guidelines for their proper usage:

5.2.1 Question Mark

When using a question mark it should be placed at the end of a sentence that is asking a direct question. The sentence should be phrased in a way that seeks information or a response.

It is important to note that indirect questions which are embedded within a sentence rather than being stand-alone questions may not always require a question mark. In such cases the sentence will end with a period instead.

Example 1: "Do you want to go to the movies?"
 - This is a direct question asking if the person wants to go to the movies. The question mark is placed at the end of the

sentence.

Example 2: "I wonder if she will come to the party."
   - This is an indirect question expressing curiosity. Since it is part of a larger sentence it does not require a question mark. The sentence ends with a period.

5.2.2 Exclamation Mark

When using an exclamation mark it should be placed at the end of a sentence that expresses strong emotion surprise or excitement. It is used to emphasize the intensity of what is being said.

It is important to avoid overusing exclamation marks as they can lose their impact if used too frequently. They are generally used sparingly in formal writing and are more commonly seen in informal or creative contexts.

Example 1: "What a beautiful day!"
   - This sentence expresses excitement and admiration for the weather and the exclamation mark emphasizes this emotion.

Example 2: "I can't believe I won the lottery!"
   - The sentence conveys a strong sense of surprise and disbelief and the exclamation mark adds emphasis to this feeling.

5.2.3 Multiple Punctuation Marks

Sometimes a sentence may require both a question mark and an exclamation mark. In such cases the order of the punctuation marks is important.

If a sentence conveys both a question and excitement or surprise the question mark should come before the exclamation mark.

Example: "You won the competition?!"
 - In this sentence the initial question is followed by an expression of astonishment. The question mark is placed before the exclamation mark to convey both the question and the excitement.

5.2.4 Capitalization and Punctuation
When using a question mark or exclamation mark the capitalization of the subsequent word or phrase depends on the grammatical structure of the sentence.

If the phrase after the question mark or exclamation mark is a complete sentence on its own it should begin with a capital letter.

Example 1: "Where did you go last night? I was looking for you."
 - The word "I" starts a new sentence after the question mark since it is a complete thought on its own.

Example 2: "What a great party! Everyone had a fantastic time."
 - "Everyone" starts a new sentence after the exclamation mark since it is a complete thought on its own.

However if the phrase after the question mark or exclamation mark is not a complete sentence it should not be capitalized.

Example 1: "Did you see the movie? it was amazing."
 - The word "it" is not capitalized since it is not the start of a

new sentence. It continues the previous sentence.

Example 2: "Wow! that car is so fast."
   - The word "that" is not capitalized since it is not the start of a new sentence. It continues the previous sentence.

In conclusion the question mark and exclamation mark play important roles in conveying questions and exclamations in written language. The question mark is used at the end of a sentence to indicate that a question is being asked while the exclamation mark is used to express strong emotion or surprise. These punctuation marks should be used correctly and placed appropriately in a sentence to ensure clarity and convey the intended meaning.

The Colon and Semi-colon

The colon and semi-colon are two punctuation marks used to enhance clarity and structure in writing. While they have distinct functions they both serve to connect ideas and create a logical flow in a sentence or sentence.

1. The Colon (:)
   The colon is primarily used to introduce a list explanation or a quote in a sentence. Here are some situations where you would use a colon:

a) To introduce a list:
   I need to buy three things from the grocery store: milk bread and eggs.

b) To introduce an explanation or clarification:
   She had one goal in mind: to win the championship.

c) To introduce a quote:
   The teacher said: "Always be prepared for the unexpected."

d) To separate titles and subtitles:
   The Great Gatsby: A Tale of Love and Betrayal.

2. The Semi-colon (;)

The semi-colon is used to connect two closely related independent clauses (complete sentences) without using a conjunction. It is often used when the two clauses are closely linked in meaning. Here are some situations where you would use a semi-colon:

a) To show a relationship between two complete thoughts:
She loves to read; her book collection is extensive.

b) To separate items in a list when the items contain commas:
The participants in the meeting included John the CEO; Sarah the CFO; and Mark the COO.

c) To clarify a complex sentence:
The test was challenging; however with enough preparation I was able to succeed.

It is important to note that both the colon and semi-colon should be used sparingly and it is essential to understand their proper usage to avoid confusion or ambiguity in your writing.

6.1 Distinguishing Between the Colon and Semi-colon:

The colon (:) and the semi-colon (;) are two punctuation marks that are often confused and misused. Understanding the difference between them is crucial for effective and correct writing.

The colon (:) has two main functions:

1. Introducing a list or series: The colon is commonly used to introduce a list of items or a series. It signals that what follows is a list or an expansion of the previous statement. For example:

- I need to buy the following items from the grocery store: milk bread eggs and butter.
    - There are three countries on my travel bucket list: Japan Italy and Australia.

2. Introducing a statement or explanation: The colon can also be used to introduce a statement or explanation that elaborates on the preceding sentence. For example:

- She had one goal in mind: to climb Mount Everest.
    - The reason for his success was simple: hard work and dedication.

On the other hand the semi-colon (;) serves as a connection between two independent clauses that are closely related in meaning. An independent clause can stand alone as a complete sentence and when connected by a semi-colon it indicates a stronger relationship between the two clauses than a period would. For example:

- John loves playing basketball; it is his favorite sport.
    - The rain stopped; the sun began to shine.

In summary the colon (:) is used to introduce lists or provide explanations while the semi-colon (;) is used to connect closely related independent clauses.

6.2 Using Colons for Lists and Introductions:

One of the main uses of the colon (:) is to introduce a list or series. It is a helpful tool for organizing information and ensuring clarity in writing. Here are a few examples of how colons can be used for lists:

Example 1: Shopping List
   I need to buy the following items from the grocery store: milk bread eggs and butter.

Example 2: Ingredients
   The recipe calls for the following ingredients: flour sugar butter and vanilla extract.

Example 3: Meeting Agenda
   The topics to be discussed in the meeting are: budget allocation marketing strategy and team performance.

In these examples the colon introduces the list of items or topics making it clear that what follows is a series of related elements.

Another use of the colon is to introduce a statement or explanation that provides further information about the preceding sentence. Here are some examples:

Example 1: Goal
   She had one goal in mind: to climb Mount Everest.

Example 2: Reason
   The reason for his success was simple: hard work and dedica-

tion.

Example 3: Conclusion

In conclusion here is what we can learn from this experience: success requires perseverance and adaptability.

In these cases the colon introduces a statement or a conclusion that elaborates on the previous sentence adding depth and clarity to the overall message.

In addition to lists and introductions colons can also be used in formal writing such as academic papers or business proposals to indicate a formal citation or reference. For example:

Example: Quotation

As Albert Einstein once said: "Imagination is more important than knowledge."

In this example the colon is used to introduce a quotation marking it as a formal reference.

It is important to note that a complete sentence should precede a colon. The sentence before the colon should be able to stand on its own and the colon should enhance or expand upon that sentence.

6.3 Utilizing Semi-colons to Connect Related Thoughts:

The semi-colon (;) is a punctuation mark that is used to connect two closely related thoughts or independent clauses. It is used to indicate a stronger relationship than a period or a comma alone.

One common use of the semi-colon is to connect two independent clauses when there is a close relationship between them. Here are some examples:

Example 1: Contrast
   She loves to dance; he prefers to sing.

Example 2: Parallel Ideas
   Mary is studying science; John is pursuing a degree in engineering.

Example 3: Cause and Effect
   He missed the train; as a result he was late for work.

In these examples the semi-colon is used to connect two independent clauses that have a logical connection or a cause-and-effect relationship.

Another common use of the semi-colon is in a list when the items within the list already contain commas. This helps to avoid confusion or ambiguity. For example:

Example: List with Commas
   The participants of the meeting included John Smith CEO; Sarah Johnson CFO; and Emily Brown CTO.

In this example the semi-colon is used to separate the list items as each item already contains a comma. This ensures clarity and makes it easier for the reader to understand the list.

It is important to note that a semi-colon should only be used when the two clauses or lists being connected are closely related in meaning. If the relationship is not strong enough it is better to use a period or a conjunction like "and" or "but" to separate the clauses.

In conclusion the semi-colon is used to connect closely related independent clauses or separate items within a list when the items themselves contain commas. It is a valuable tool for achieving clarity and coherence in writing.

Quotation Marks

7.1 Indicating Direct Speech and Quotations

Quotation marks are punctuation marks used to indicate direct speech and quotations. They are primarily used to enclose the exact words spoken or written by someone else. Quotation marks are essential in writing to differentiate between your own words and the words of others. They help provide clarity and accuracy in the representation of someone's speech or writing.

In general there are two main types of quotation marks: single quotation marks (') and double quotation marks ("). The choice between using single or double quotation marks may depend on the specific style guide or preference of the writer.

Direct speech is usually enclosed within double quotation marks. For example:

John said "I am going to the store."

In this example the exact words spoken by John are enclosed within double quotation marks to indicate direct speech. The reader understands that these are the words spoken by John.

Quotation marks are also used when including a direct quote from a text or other written material. For example:

According to the article "The economy is experiencing significant growth."

In this example the quote from the article is enclosed within double quotation marks to indicate that these are the exact words from the published article. This helps to attribute the quote correctly and avoid plagiarism.

When quoting a longer passage or multiple paragraphs some style guides may require using block quotations. Block quotations are indented single-spaced and do not require the use of quotation marks. A citation is usually provided at the end of the block quote. For example:

In his famous speech Martin Luther King Jr. said:

"I have a dream that one day this nation will rise up and live out the true meaning of its creed: 'We hold these truths to be self-evident: that all men are created equal.'

I have a dream that one day on the red hills of Georgia the sons of former slaves and the sons of former slave owners will be able to sit down together at a table of brotherhood."

In this example the entire passage from Martin Luther King Jr.'s speech is indented and presented as a block quote. The absence of quotation marks signifies that the passage is a direct quote and the citation is provided at the end.

7.2 Punctuating Quotes within Quotes

Sometimes you may encounter a situation where you need to include a quote within a quote. In such cases it is important to properly punctuate the quotes to ensure clarity and accuracy.

When a quote within a quote is introduced it is enclosed within single quotation marks. For example:

John said "Samantha told me 'I will be there on time.'"

In this example John is reporting what Samantha said. John's own words are enclosed within double quotation marks while Samantha's words are enclosed within single quotation marks.

If there is another quote within the quote within a quote it follows the same pattern. The innermost quote is enclosed within double quotation marks while the next level of quoting is enclosed within single quotation marks. For example:

John said "Samantha told me 'Sarah said "I can't make it."'"

In this example John is reporting what Samantha said about Sarah. John's own words are enclosed within double quotation marks Samantha's words are enclosed within single quotation marks and Sarah's words are enclosed within double quotation marks again.

It is important to maintain the proper order of single and double quotation marks to avoid confusion.

Another important aspect of punctuating quotes within quotes is the use of punctuation marks. The punctuation marks within the innermost quote fall within the single quotation marks. For example:

John said "Samantha told me 'Wake up!'"

In this example the exclamation mark is within the single quotation marks because it is part of Samantha's speech not John's reporting.

However if the punctuation mark belongs to the outer quote it falls outside of the single quotation marks. For example:

John said "Samantha told me 'Wake up'!"

In this example the exclamation mark belongs to John's reporting not Samantha's speech.

It is important to pay attention to the placement of punctuation marks to accurately represent the intended meaning.

In summary quotation marks are used to indicate direct speech and quotations. They help distinguish between the words of the author and the words of others. Direct speech and quotations are usually enclosed within double quotation marks while quotes within quotes are enclosed within single quotation marks. Proper punctuation within the quotes is also crucial to convey the intended meaning accurately.

The Dash and Hyphen

The dash and the hyphen are punctuation marks used in writing to indicate breaks or connections between words or phrases. While they may appear similar, they serve different purposes.

1. The Dash (—): The dash is a longer horizontal line used to set off or emphasize certain elements within a sentence. There are two types of dashes: the en dash and the em dash.

- En dash (–): The en dash is slightly longer than a hyphen and is used to indicate a range or connection between two elements. For example, "pages 10–15" denotes pages 10 to 15, or "the New York–London flight" signifies a flight between New York and London.

- Em dash (—): The em dash is longer than both the hyphen and the en dash. It is primarily used to create a strong break or interruption in a sentence. Em dashes are often employed to set off a parenthetical phrase, an abrupt change in thought, or an emphasis on a particular point. For instance, "The concert was incredible—everyone was talking about it for weeks!" In this case, the em dash emphasizes the impact of the concert.

2. The Hyphen (-): The hyphen is a shorter horizontal line used to join words together and form compound words or compound modifiers. It can be used to connect two or more words to create a single, unified concept. Examples include "mother-in-law," "well-known," or "high-speed." The hyphen can also be used to break a word at the end of a line when there isn't enough space for the whole word.

It's important to note that the en dash, em dash, and hyphen have specific typographical rules and style conventions associated with their usage, which may vary across different style guides or writing contexts.

8.1 Understanding the Different Functions of Dashes and Hyphens:

Dashes and hyphens are two important punctuation marks that are often confused with each other. While they may look similar they serve different purposes and should be used correctly in writing. Understanding the functions of dashes and hyphens can help improve clarity and ensure proper usage.

A hyphen (-) is used to join words or parts of words together. It is primarily used to form compound words and to divide words at the end of a line. Let's take a look at some examples:

- Compound Words:
    - blue-green
    - well-known
    - self-confidence

In these examples the hyphen is used to combine two or more words into a single word to create new meanings. It helps clarify the relationship between the words and avoids confusion. For example "blue-green" refers to a color that is a combination of blue and green while "well-known" means widely recognized or famous.

- Division at the End of a Line:
    - The cat was play-
    ing in the garden.

In this example the hyphen is used to divide the word "playing" at the end of a line when it doesn't fit entirely. This is done to maintain readability and avoid awkward spacing.

On the other hand a dash (—) is used to emphasize information or to set off interruptions within a sentence. It is longer than a hyphen and can be used in two different forms: the em dash and the en dash. Let's explore these uses in more detail in the next section.

8.2 Emphasizing Information and Setting Off Interruptions:

The dash is a versatile punctuation mark that can be used to give emphasis to certain information or to set off interruptions within a sentence. It adds a sense of drama immediacy or importance to the content. There are two common uses of dashes: the em dash (—) and the en dash (–).

- Em Dash (—):
    The em dash is the longer dash also known as the "double

dash." It is called an "em" dash because its length is equal to the width of the letter "M" in a particular typeface. The em dash is primarily used for emphasis or to set off interrupting or explanatory information within a sentence.

1. Emphasizing Information:
   - My mother gave me three options for dinner—pizza pasta or salad.
   - The storm was unpredictable—rain thunder and lightning filled the sky.

In these examples the em dash is used to emphasize the options or the chaotic nature of the storm. It draws attention to the information and highlights its significance.

2. Setting Off Interruptions:
   - The party—despite the rain—was a huge success.
   - The professor—known for his strictness—gave everyone an extension on the assignment.

In these examples the em dash is used to set off interruptions or additional information that is not essential to the main clause. It serves as a way to add extra details or explanations without disrupting the flow of the sentence.

- En Dash (–):
   The en dash is the shorter dash named after its length being equal to the width of the letter "N" in a particular typeface. It is primarily used to indicate a range or connection between two things such as numbers dates or locations.

1. Indicating a Range:
    - Pages 15–20 of the book provide detailed instructions.
    - The conference will take place from July 10–12 in New York.

In these examples the en dash is used to show a span or range of pages dates or times. It helps clarify the relationship between the two endpoints and avoids ambiguity.

2. Indicating Connection or Attribution:
    - The Paris–London flight was delayed due to bad weather.
    - The book was written by John Smith–a renowned author.

In these examples the en dash is used to denote a connection or attribution between two elements. It shows their relationship and avoids confusion.

Overall understanding the different functions of dashes and hyphens is crucial for clear and effective writing. Hyphens are used to join words or parts of words to create compound words or to divide words at the end of a line. Dashes on the other hand are used to emphasize information or to set off interruptions within a sentence. The em dash is used for emphasis and interruption while the en dash is used for indicating range or connection. Correct usage of dashes and hyphens can greatly improve the clarity and readability of your writing.

Parentheses and Brackets

Parentheses and brackets are punctuation marks used to enclose and separate elements within a written text. They serve different purposes and have distinct characteristics.

Parentheses, also known as round brackets or simply brackets, are represented by "(" and ")". They are used to insert additional information, explanations, or asides within a sentence. The content enclosed in parentheses is considered non-essential to the main sentence but provides supplementary details or clarifications. These additional elements can be removed, and the sentence will still make sense grammatically.

For example:
   - The concert (which was held last night) was amazing.
   - The company is expanding its operations (including opening new branches).

Brackets can also be used to group mathematical expressions, indicating priority or order of operations in mathematical equations. For example: $(3 + 5) \times 2$.

On the other hand, brackets, also known as square brackets,

are represented by "[" and "]". They are primarily used to add explanatory or editorial information to a quotation or to clarify a statement. Brackets are often employed when modifying a quote by inserting words or phrases to provide context or to correct grammar.

For example:
- "The witness stated, '[The suspect] appeared nervous.'"
- "She [the teacher] emphasized the importance of studying."

Brackets can also be used in certain writing styles or formats, such as in citations or references, to indicate optional or alternative elements.

In summary, parentheses (round brackets) are used to include additional information or asides within a sentence, while brackets (square brackets) are used for adding explanatory information to quotations or modifying them. Both serve to enhance understanding or provide additional context to the reader.

9.1 Enclosing Additional Information and Clarifications:

Parentheses and brackets are often used to enclose additional information or clarifications within a sentence. This additional information can help provide context or explanation for the main idea of the sentence.

For example:
1. "I am going to visit my friend (who lives in New York) next week."

In this sentence the phrase "who lives in New York" is enclosed in parentheses to provide additional information about the friend. It is not essential to the main idea of the sentence but provides extra details.

2. "The event will take place on Friday (October 20th)."
Here the date "October 20th" is enclosed in parentheses to specify the exact day of the event.

3. "She enjoys playing soccer (especially on sunny days)."
In this sentence the phrase "especially on sunny days" is enclosed in parentheses to show that it is an additional detail about her enjoyment of playing soccer.

The use of parentheses can also be seen in academic writing where additional information or explanations are often provided. For example:

"The study conducted by Johnson (2018) found a significant correlation between sleep deprivation and decreased cognitive function."

In this sentence the year "2018" is enclosed in parentheses to indicate the source of the study conducted by Johnson.

Brackets on the other hand are used to enclose additional information within a quotation or to clarify and modify a quoted statement.

For example:

"He [the president] addressed the nation on the issue of climate change."

In this sentence the phrase "the president" is enclosed in brackets to provide clarification about who "He" refers to.

Another example:

"The witness stated 'I saw him [the suspect] running away from the crime scene.'"

Here the phrase "the suspect" is enclosed in brackets to clarify the pronoun "him".

9.2 Using Brackets for Editorial Clarifications:

Brackets are often used in writing and editing to provide clarifications or corrections to quoted material. When quoting someone else's words it is sometimes necessary to make changes for clarity or to correct grammar errors. In these cases brackets are used to indicate the alterations made.

For example:

Original quote: "She don't [doesn't] like chocolate."

Corrected quote: "She [doesn't] like chocolate."

In this example brackets are used to indicate that the incorrect word "don't" has been changed to "doesn't" to match the correct grammar.

Brackets can also be used to indicate the omission of words or phrases from a quotation. This is often done to shorten the quote or remove irrelevant information while still maintaining the meaning.

For example:

Original quote: "The researchers found that the results were statistically significant among both men and women regardless of age."

Shortened quote: "The researchers found that the results were statistically significant among [both men and women] regardless of age."

In this example the phrase "both men and women" has been placed in brackets to indicate that it has been omitted from the shortened quote.

Brackets can also be used to provide contextual information within a quotation especially when the original text is ambiguous or unclear.

For example:

Original quote: "The professor stated 'It is not necessary [for you] to attend the lecture.'"

In this example the phrase "for you" is placed in brackets to clarify the intended meaning of the professor's statement. This addition helps to provide context that may not be evident in the original quote.

In conclusion parentheses and brackets are used in writing to enclose additional information provide clarifications or make changes to quoted material. Parentheses are used to provide extra details or explanations within a sentence while brackets are used for editorial clarifications and modifications within a quotation. Understanding the proper use of parentheses and brackets can help improve the clarity and accuracy of your writing.

The Ellipsis

The ellipsis represented by three consecutive periods (...) or by a single character (... is a punctuation mark used to indicate the omission of words phrases or sentences in a written text. It is often used in both formal and informal writing to convey a sense of omission or trail-off.

The ellipsis is used when a writer wants to show that some words or information have been deliberately left out of a quotation or a sentence. This can be done to avoid repetition condense a lengthy quote or simply to indicate that something is missing.

For example consider the following sentence:
    Original sentence: "I visited the park the zoo and the museum on my trip."
    Sentence with ellipsis: "I visited the park...on my trip."

In this example the writer chose to omit the mention of the zoo and the museum from the sentence using an ellipsis to show the omission. This can also be used in longer quotes where only a portion is relevant to the context.

The ellipsis is also used to indicate a trailing off or hesitation in speech or thought. It suggests that the speaker or writer has more to say but is intentionally leaving it unsaid or unfinished. This can be used to create a sense of suspense mystery or to invoke the reader's imagination.

For example consider the following sentence:
  "I had so much to say but... never mind forget it."

In this example the ellipsis is used to show the speaker cutting off their thought implying that there is more they could say but choose not to.

It is important to note that while the ellipsis is a useful tool for conveying omission and trail-off in writing it should be used judiciously and in accordance with the rules of grammar and style guides. Overuse of ellipses can disrupt the flow of a text or create confusion for the reader.

200 Examples

Here are 200 examples of the use of punctuation in English:

1. The cat is black.
2. I love pizza!
3. It's raining outside.
4. Can you pass me the salt, please?
5. She said, "I can't do it."
6. Are you coming to the party?
7. The movie was amazing!
8. John and Sarah went to the store.
9. Excuse me; can I ask you a question?
10. I need to buy eggs, milk, and bread.
11. He shouted, "Get out of here!"
12. The dog wagged its tail.
13. The train arrives at 9:30 a.m.
14. Wow, what a beautiful sunset!
15. "I'm sorry," she whispered.
16. The book is on the table.
17. I can't believe it's already July!
18. The concert starts at 7 o'clock.
19. Stop! Don't go any further.

20. She has three siblings: two sisters and a brother.
21. "How are you today?" he asked.
22. The car honked its horn loudly.
23. Have a nice day!
24. The baby's first word was "mama."
25. I don't want to go to school.
26. The cake is delicious.
27. "I'm so tired," she yawned.
28. He arrived late; everyone was waiting.
29. Can you swim?
30. Please, be quiet!
31. The phone rang incessantly.
32. I can't find my keys anywhere.
33. "Goodbye," he said sadly.
34. I saw a shooting star!
35. The computer crashed; I lost all my work.
36. Don't forget to bring your umbrella.
37. The baby cried all night long.
38. My favorite color is blue.
39. "I won the lottery!" he exclaimed.
40. They went to the beach and had a picnic.
41. I'm going to the gym, and then I'll grab dinner.
42. The movie starts at 8 p.m., so we should leave soon.
43. The sun is shining brightly today.
44. The dog barked loudly.
45. "How was your day?" she asked eagerly.
46. I need to buy new shoes, a jacket, and a hat.
47. He smiled and waved at me.
48. It's been a long day; I need some rest.
49. Can you lend me a pen, please?
50. The cat meowed softly.

51. "What time is it?" she wondered.
52. I'm sorry for being late.
53. The bookshelf is full of books.
54. The fireworks lit up the sky.
55. She wore a beautiful dress to the party.
56. "Happy birthday!" they sang.
57. I can't wait to see you!
58. The car screeched to a halt.
59. My parents went on vacation without me.
60. The movie was suspenseful and thrilling.
61. "Do you want some coffee?" he asked.
62. He opened the door slowly.
63. She ran as fast as she could.
64. The cat purred contentedly.
65. I finished my homework on time.
66. "I'm sorry, but I can't make it," she replied.
67. The bell rang, signaling the end of class.
68. The fire crackled in the fireplace.
69. She smiled and hugged me tightly.
70. The train departed from the station.
71. "I love you," he whispered in her ear.
72. The storm was fierce and destructive.
73. Please, help me!
74. The music played softly in the background.
75. They danced under the moonlight.
76. The baby giggled with joy.
77. "Where are you going?" she asked.
78. He jumped with excitement.
79. The clock ticked slowly.
80. The museum is closed on Mondays.
81. I can't believe I passed the exam!

82. "Wait for me!" she shouted.
83. The river flowed gently.
84. The horse galloped across the field.
85. The concert was canceled due to bad weather.
86. "Congratulations on your promotion!" they cheered.
87. The children laughed and played together.
88. She painted a beautiful landscape.
89. "I can't do this anymore," he sighed.
90. The butterfly fluttered its wings gracefully.
91. Please, don't leave me alone.
92. The wind blew fiercely.
93. "What's your favorite movie?" she asked curiously.
94. He climbed to the top of the mountain.
95. The airplane soared through the clouds.
96. The cake tasted delicious.
97. "Can you help me with this puzzle?" he asked.
98. The moon shone brightly in the night sky.
99. The birds chirped happily in the trees.
100. She whispered a secret in my ear.
101. "I'm really sorry," she apologized.
102. The car engine roared loudly.
103. The baby slept peacefully through the night.
104. "Where have you been?" he questioned.
105. The raindrops fell gently on the roof.
106. The children ran and played in the park.
107. "I'm here for you," she reassured.
108. The thunder rumbled in the distance.
109. The cake was decorated with colorful sprinkles.
110. "I don't understand," he confessed.
111. The leaves rustled in the wind.
112. The dog wagged its tail happily.

113. "I missed you," she admitted.
114. The ice cream melted quickly in the sun.
115. The car honked angrily at the slow driver.
116. The baby crawled towards its favorite toy.
117. "Are you ready?" he asked impatiently.
118. The waves crashed against the shore.
119. The butterfly landed delicately on the flower.
120. "I'll be there soon," she promised.
121. The clock struck midnight.
122. The children screamed with delight on the roller coaster.
123. "I need a break," he pleaded.
124. The rain stopped, and a rainbow appeared.
125. The fire crackled and warmed the room.
126. "Why did you do that?" she demanded.
127. The snowflakes fell softly from the sky.
128. The dog barked fiercely at the intruder.
129. "I'm so proud of you," he beamed.
130. The boat sailed gracefully across the lake.
131. The sun set behind the mountains.
132. "Can you pass me the remote?" he asked.
133. The baby laughed uncontrollably at the funny faces.
134. "I'll never forget this moment," she reminisced.
135. The wind howled through the trees.
136. The children skipped and jumped in the playground.
137. "I can't believe you did that!" he exclaimed.
138. The flowers bloomed beautifully in the garden.
139. The car screeched and came to a stop.
140. "Are you okay?" she inquired with concern.
141. The leaves changed color in the fall.
142. The horse neighed and galloped away.
143. "I'm not sure," he pondered.

144. The rain washed away the dirt from the sidewalk.

145. The fire crackled, providing warmth and light

146. "What's your favorite book?" she asked with curiosity.

147. The birds sang melodiously in the morning.

148. The car engine purred smoothly.

149. "I'll never forgive you," he said angrily.

150. The waves crashed against the rocky shore.

151. The butterfly fluttered away, disappearing into the distance.

152. "Can you please close the window?" she requested.

153. The snow covered the ground, creating a winter wonderland.

154. The children whispered secrets to each other.

155. "I'm really sorry for what I did," she apologized sincerely.

156. The thunder boomed, rattling the windows.

157. The dog whimpered, seeking comfort from its owner.

158. "Where are you going?" he questioned with curiosity.

159. The leaves swirled in the autumn breeze.

160. The baby gurgled happily, playing with its toys.

161. "I'm so excited!" she exclaimed with enthusiasm.

162. The rain poured heavily, drenching everything in its path.

163. The fire crackled and popped, creating a cozy atmosphere.

164. "What's your favorite color?" he asked playfully.

165. The birds flew gracefully across the sky.

166. The car screeched around the sharp corner.

167. "Are you sure about this?" she asked uncertainly.

168. The leaves crunched underfoot as they walked through the forest.

169. The dog growled menacingly, protecting its territory.

170. "I can't believe we made it!" he exclaimed breathlessly.

171. The waves gently lapped against the sandy beach.

172. The butterfly landed delicately on the tip of a flower petal.

173. "I'll be there in a minute," she called from the other room.

174. The clock chimed, marking the passage of time.

175. The children giggled and laughed, filled with joy.

176. "I need a vacation," he sighed wearily.

177. The raindrops tapped rhythmically on the roof.

178. The fire crackled, casting dancing shadows on the walls.

179. "Why did you say that?" she questioned with confusion.

180. The snowflakes drifted lazily from the sky.

181. The dog barked excitedly, wagging its tail.

182. "I'm so happy for you," he said with a smile.

183. The boat sailed smoothly across the calm waters.

184. The sun dipped below the horizon, painting the sky with hues of pink and orange.

185. "Can you please turn up the volume?" he asked politely.

186. The baby cooed softly, enjoying the attention.

187. "I'll always treasure this memory," she said wistfully.

188. The wind whistled through the trees, creating an eerie sound.

189. The children laughed and played, their innocence shining through.

190. "I can't believe you did that!" he exclaimed in disbelief.

191. The flowers swayed in the gentle breeze.

192. The car screeched to a halt, narrowly avoiding a collision.

193. "Are you feeling better?" she asked with concern.

194. The leaves crunched under their feet as they walked along the trail.

195. The horse neighed, eager to gallop freely.

196. "I'm not sure I understand," he admitted, furrowing his

brow.

197. The rain washed away the dirt, leaving everything fresh and clean.

198. The fire crackled, providing both warmth and a mesmerizing sight.

199. "What's your favorite movie genre?" she asked, hoping for a recommendation.

200. The birds chirped cheerfully, announcing the arrival of spring.